Snowboarding

Sandra Woodcock

Published in association with The Basic Skills Agency

Hodder & Stoughton

A MEMBER OF THE HODDER HEADLINE GROUP

Acknowledgements

Cover: Getty Images/Digitalvision

Photos: pp. iv, 3, 24 Action-Plus Photographic; pp. 8, 19 © Allsport; p. 13 Gonzalo M. Azumendi; p. 17 Vandystadt Agence de Presse/Allsport; p. 27 Ski Village, Sheffield.

Orders: please contact Bookpoint Ltd, 130 Milton Park, Abingdon, Oxon OX14 4SB. Telephone: (44) 01235 827720, Fax: (44) 01235 400454. Lines are open from 9.00–6.00, Monday to Saturday, with a 24 hour message answering service. You can also order through our website www.hodderheadline.co.uk

British Library Cataloguing in Publication Data
A catalogue record for this title is available from The British Library

ISBN 0 340 87696 4

First published 1999
This edition published 2003
Impression number   10 9 8 7 6 5 4 3 2 1
Year   2007 2006 2005 2004 2003

Copyright © 1999 Sandra Woodcock

Typeset by Fakenham Photosetting Ltd, Fakenham, Norfolk.
Printed in Great Britain for Hodder & Stoughton Educational, a division of Hodder Headline, 338 Euston Road, London NW1 3BH by The Bath Press, Bath.

Contents

1 What is Surfing?

Surfing is all about riding waves.
The waves can be huge and powerful or small.
You can use a board or just your body.
But the aim is the same.
A surfer wants to feel part of the wave.
He wants to move with the water
as it crashes onto the shore
and to feel the power of the sea.

As a wave comes into the shore,
you can see it swell.
A crest forms and you see a hollow tube.
Then it breaks into a mass of white water.

The aim is to try to ride
on the front of the wave
as it speeds to the shore.
Strong swimmers can swim out past the surf
and catch a wave as it peaks.
Weak swimmers can wait
to catch the wave, just after it breaks.

The best waves for surfing break onto
long gently sloping beaches.

If you are on a good beach
with waves that are not too high,
you can try bodysurfing.
This is like surfing without a board.
You just let the wave carry you in.

Most people start off by buying a bodyboard.
In bodyboarding a small board is used.
You hold onto the sides of the board
and press it close to your chest.
Your legs should be clear of the board
and can be used for steering.
Bodyboarders always wear flippers
to get up speed to catch the wave.

You catch a wave by paddling ahead of it.
When the surf catches up with you,
you stop paddling, hang on
and are carried to the shore.

In gentle surf, bodyboarding can be a stage
in learning longboard surfing.
But in high surf,
bodyboarding is more difficult
and is a sport in its own right.

The longboard surfer catches a wave
in the same way.
But as soon as he joins it,
he holds the edges of the board
and tries to stand.
He then has to control the board
by moving his body weight.

Trying to catch a wave.

2 Skills

Good surfers change speed and direction
by walking on the board.
If they seem to be losing their balance,
they drop to their knees again.

Surfers can ride the wave
in a straight line to the beach,
or they can turn left or right.
Some surfers like to do tricks
to show off their skills.
They do handstands
or somersaults on the board.

Big waves curl over before they break.
You can see a hollow tube under the curl.
Some surfers like to surf through this.
It's like being in a tunnel
with the wave above you.
Some people call it 'tube riding'.
Others call it 'getting barrelled'.

Good surfers can do fast turns
and stay with the wave for the longest time.
They look as if they are dancing on the sea.

Surfers always want to ride
bigger and better waves.
The best places to surf are Hawaii, Fiji and Bali,
Australia and Mexico.
The highest waves for surfing are in Hawaii.
They often reach between 9 and 10 metres.
The longest ride on a sea wave
is about 1,700 metres.
These waves are found in
Mantanchen Bay in Mexico.

Australia has fantastic surfing beaches.
The best one is Bell's Beach in Victoria.
Many international competitions are held here.
California also has many surfing beaches.
Huntington Beach in California is one of
the oldest surfing centres.
Many big events take place there.

Mexico also has good surfing beaches.
It's great to surf in hot countries
with blue sky and lots of sun.
But surfing can be done all over the world.
Biarritz in France is
Europe's most popular beach.
In Britain you can surf on many coasts.
Newquay, in Cornwall is Britain's
favourite surf beach.

If there is good surf you will find surfers:
from the warm sea of the Caribbean
to the Cold Atlantic;
from Hawaii to North Scotland.

3 The Gear

If you are lucky and can surf in warm water –
at least 20°C – you won't need a wetsuit.
If the water temperature is between 18–20°C
you will need a spring wetsuit.
This has no sleeves
and is cut off at the knee.
A winter wetsuit for colder water
has full arms and legs.

Wetsuits are made of neoprene.
In cold water, surfers wear
neoprene hoods and gloves.
They also wear boots
to protect their feet from cold,
sharp rocks and shells.
If there are rocks or reefs,
surfers should wear a helmet.

At first, boards were made of wood.
Only very strong people could handle them.
Modern boards are made
from fibreglass and styrofoam.
There are different kinds of boards.

When you begin, it's best to get a short wide board
(50–58 cm at the middle).
The front end or nose should be round.
This type of board is called a shortboard.
Shortboards come in all shapes and sizes.
They can be up to 3 metres long.
When you have had some practice,
you will probably want a narrower shortboard.

Longboards are between 2½ and 3½ metres.
They are sometimes called Malibus.
They are thicker
and it's harder to handle them
if the surf is big.

Performance boards are shaped to be faster.
There are short and long boards like this.
Surfers use the board
that suits the waves they like to ride.

Big Guns are boards for experts.
They are long, narrow and fast.
They are for big waves
ranging from 4 metres to over 6 metres.

Modern surfboards have colourful designs.
They look like works of art.
Some surfers give their boards names.

Surfers keep hold of their boards
with a leash, so they don't lose them.
They also have to wax their boards
to stop them slipping off
when they stand on the board
to catch a wave.

4 Getting Started

If you want to learn to surf,
it is important to be a good swimmer.
Don't depend on your board to keep you safe.
Swimming on a surf beach is not the same
as in a swimming pool!
If you are not fit, you will soon get tired.
Surfing is hard work as well as good fun!

Always make sure you are on a safe beach
and that there are other people around.
If there are good surfers in the water,
keep out of their way
until you feel confident.

Watch the sea.
It's good to know how
a wave behaves before you try it.
Does it break to the left or to the right?
When you go into the water,
the board should be by the side of your body.
If the board is in front of you,
a wave could pick it up and slam it into you.

At first, it's best to ride the board
on your stomach.
You can paddle through the breaking waves
to get used to it.

Then you can try standing up.
To do this, you need to be ahead of a wave.
As you paddle,
you feel the wave pick up the board.
As it gets faster, push up into a crouch.
Then lean and turn into the wave.
All surfers wipeout.
This means you come off the board
and the wave goes over you.
Don't panic.
Get away from the board
so that it doesn't hit you.
Be ready to hold your breath.
Under the water, cover your head
with your arms, until you are out again.

5 Competitions

Some surfers love surfing for its own sake.
Others like to compete.
There are competitions for amateurs
and for professionals.
Some of the top surfers include
the American, Kelly Slater,
and the Australians, Tom Curren, Tom Carroll
and Mark Occhilupo.
Australian Lisa Anderson
is one of the top women surfers.
She has been world champion.

Professional surfers are paid by sponsors.
They are paid to travel the world,
surfing the best waves.
It sounds like a dream!
If you want to be a professional,
you need a record of competing.

In competitions, there is a panel of judges.
They give marks for skills,
such as turns and barrels or tube rides.
They give marks for style and timing.

Each surfer has to ride a number of waves.
Each wave ride is marked.
The best three or four waves
are added up to give a final score.

There are many world events.
They are sponsored by surf companies
such as Billabong, Rip Curl and Quiksilver
or companies like Coca-Cola.

One of the biggest surf events in the world
is the US Open held at Huntington Beach.
It lasts for a week.
In 1997, 700 people took part
and there were 250,000 spectators.
World champion surfer Kelly Slater was there.
He has five world titles.
There were young surfers, too,
like Bobby Martinez who was only 16.
The Pipeline competition in Hawaii
is another important competition.

Surfing has been around for a very long time.
But it has never been in the Olympic Games.
Now that is going to change.
Surfing will be shown at the Olympic Games
for the first time in Sydney in the year 2000.
It will be a full Olympic Sport in the year 2004.

There are many competitions for surfers
throughout the world.

6 What is Snowboarding?

Think about surfing on snow.
That's snowboarding.
Snowboarding is a new and exciting sport.
It's a sport for young people who like snow
and mountains and something different.
Like skiing, it's a way of getting around,
and having some fun on snowy mountain slopes.

Many people have tried using
a single board on snow.
In 1965 an American called Sherman Poppen
made a toy for his children.
He called it a 'Snurfer'.
It was like two skis fixed together.

In 1970, in the mountains of North America,
a young man called Milovich and his friends
were enjoying the snow.
In the summer they were surfers in California,
but now they were trying out their surfing skills
on the snow.
They used tea trays from the mountain cafe!
This is how snowboarding started.
It was a way of surfing the snow.

7 Snowboarding Hits the Ski Slopes

People began to try making proper snowboards.
Mike Olsen was one of the first to do this.
In the 1980s the Burton company
developed and made snowboards.
In 1982 the first international snowboard race
was held in Vermont USA.

But there was a problem.
The best place to snowboard
is on a snowy mountain.
The best places are already ski resorts.
The ski resorts did not welcome snowboarders.

People said snowboarding was not a proper sport.
It had no rules, no one had control of it.
That was why so many young people liked it!
The ski resorts would not allow snowboarding.
It upset the skiers.
But the snowboarders went anyway.
More people began to try it.
Young children, whose parents were skiing,
saw snowboards and wanted to try them.

Skiing can be hard to learn.
But many young people already had
the skills for snowboarding.
They had done skateboarding at home.
Snowboarding looked great fun
and not too hard to do.

The sport started to take off in a big way.
Most ski resorts
began to cater for snowboarders.
After all, some of the skiers were trying it
and liking it too!

For skiing, it's best to have hard icy snow.
On days when the snow is slushy or powdery,
it's not good for skiing.
But it is ideal for snowboarding.
So people could do both.

In 1998, for the first time,
snowboarding was in the Winter Olympics.
Now it is seen as a sport in its own right.
There are still more skiers
than snowboarders on the slopes.
But in the next 10 years
that is likely to change.

The French snowboarding team.
Snowboarding is now a sport in its own right.

8 How is it Done?

Snowboarding is riding the snow.
There are two main ways of doing this.
One way is called 'free riding'.
There is nothing special about this style.
It just means going in one direction,
and doing basic turns.
It's just doing what you like
in your own way –
simply enjoying the snow.

The moves may be simple,
but free riding can be exciting.
There can be steep slopes and forest tracks.
Free riding away from the ski routes
can be dangerous.
It's exciting making your own route
but you need your wits about you.

'Extreme' snowboarding means
free riding the most dangerous parts
of the mountain.
It needs special skills.

'Freestyling' is different.
This means doing tricks
and stunts with the snowboard.
You can twist, jump and somersault.
It's like skateboarding,
but the ramps are on the mountains.

A 'half pipe' is a man-made ramp
shaped like a U.
Snowboarders ride up the sides,
jumping in and out and doing tricks.
You need very good skills for this.
It helps if you have no fear!

9 The Gear

There are different types of snowboard.
When you choose a board,
you need to think about how tall you are
and how much you weigh.
You also need to know
what kind of snowboarding you are going to do.

Free ride boards are narrow and stiff.
The nose (front) of the board
is turned up, so it will move easily
through powder snow.

Freestyle boards are wider and softer.
The nose and tail are the same shape.
This means you can ride
both backwards and forwards.

Racing boards are very narrow and stiff.
The tail is flat because
they are only meant to go forwards.

It is important to have the right boots.
They must fit well and be comfortable
for what you want to do.

Some boots are hard like ski boots.
They need bindings and clips.
You can also get 'step in' boots.
For freestyling, it is better
to have soft boots with laces or velcro.
For racing, it is better
to have hard boots.

Snowboarders wear casual loose clothes
like skate wear.
Trousers have extra padding
in the seat and in the knees.
You should wear several layers
and the top layer needs to be snowproof.
Snowboarders wear gloves
with high cuffs, to keep out the snow.
A woolly hat will keep your head warm.
It's also important to wear goggles
to protect your eyes from the sun.

It's not cheap to get started in snowboarding.
Even the most basic beginner's board
is quite expensive.
But many shops sell second-hand gear.
Snowboarders update their gear quite often.
So there's lots of good gear
to buy second hand.

10 Getting Started

Many people start snowboarding
by just having a go.
Anyone who has done skateboarding
or surfing, soon learns free riding.
The whole point about free riding
is to do it your way.
People who have no boarding skills
may need a few lessons to get started.

The first thing to work out
is how to stand on the board.
Some people like to have
their right foot forward.
This is called 'goofy' or 'reverse', as in surfing.
Putting the left foot forward
is called 'regular' or 'normal'.
The top half of the body and the hips
face the same way as the front foot.

One edge of the board should grip the snow.
You get down the slope by turning,
first one way and then the other.

To turn the board
you have to lean back on your heels
or lean forward towards your toes.
As the weight of your body shifts,
it steers the board.

Beginners are sure to fall over quite a lot.
On snow this doesn't hurt too much.
When you go onto a snow slope
for the first time,
it's easy to make mistakes.
If you put the snowboard down
and let go of it,
it will shoot off by itself
and may hit someone.
You should have a leash
to fix the board to your boot.
Then if you fall over
and let go of the board,
it stays with you.

A snowboarder makes a jump.

When you feel confident with the basics,
you may want to try some tricks.
It's best to start with a simple jump.
To do this, you lean back
and push with the back foot
to get you off the ground.
When you are in the air,
you can pull up your legs under you.
You should land with your weight
over the middle of the board.
This simple jump is called an Ollie.
Next you can try to grab
some part of the board as you jump.

11 What if there is no Snow?

Snowboarding without snow
sounds like nonsense.
But many snowboarders
can't get to the snow very often.
The sport is doing well
in many places without much snow.

People learn their skills on dry slopes.
A few places have indoor slopes
with real snow.
But most have plastic surfaces.
It's hard to learn on plastic.
It hurts when you fall over.
Some people have broken their fingers
in gaps on the slope.

There can be a lot of falling over
and getting up again.
Then suddenly it clicks
and you can do it.

It's not the same as snow
but when you have paid
a lot of money for your gear,
you want to use it more
than a few weeks in the year.
So there is a snowboarding scene
in many countries without much snow
and more people are joining the sport
all the time.

12 Competitions

Snowboarding became an Olympic Sport in 1998.
But well before that, there were
international competitions in snowboarding.

Snowboarders who want to turn professional
get sponsors to pay them.
One big sponsor is The Burton Corporation
which makes snowboarding clothes
and equipment.

When snowboarding became an Olympic sport,
it was seen as a branch of skiing.
The events were the same as ski events –
Slalom and Grand Slalom and downhill races.

But it is a new sport and snowboarders want
to set their own style in competitions too.
Some people say the competitions should test
the skills and flair in snowboarding,
not how fast someone can go.

Some snowboarders say it would be better
if the sport stayed out of the Olympics.
Then it would keep its spirit of freedom.